AMAZING LOVE
Rosary Meditations
For Teens

Mari Seaberg, Adrian Inclan & Maria Boas
Illustrations by Maria Boas

Caritas Press, USA

AMAZING LOVE
Rosary Meditations for Teens

Mari Seaberg, Adrian Inclan, & Maria Boas
Illustrations by Maria Boas

Edited by Sherry Boas

For information regarding permission, contact Sherry@LilyTrilogy.com

First Edition

10 9 8 7 6 5 4 3 2 1

ISBN 978-1-940209-00-5

For reorders, visit LilyTrilogy.com or CatholicWord.com
Sherry@LilyTrilogy.com

Published by Caritas Press, Arizona, USA

For my parents, who instilled the faith in me, taught me to follow and trust Christ and showed me how to be a good Christian through every high and low.

---Adrian I.

For Frank Cicero, an amazing person whose patience and piety encourage me to live out my Christian vocation with vigor and devotion.

---Maria B.

For my parents, who provide me with a beautiful model of Christian love and always encourage me to deepen my faith.

---Mari S.

INTRODUCTION

The Rosary provides a way for us to make the world a better place. Amazingly, this ancient prayer can change the future. If we pray the Rosary faithfully and strive to live what we have learned, we will grow to love Jesus more, and loving Him means loving everyone God places in our lives. We will grow to love the Mass more because we will see unfolding at the altar all the things we have prayed through the Rosary. Our Lady asks everyone to pray the Rosary every day to combat the evils of this world.

St. Louis de Montfort said that praying the Rosary devoutly dons Jesus and Mary with crowns of red and white roses that never fade or whither. The word rosary means "crown of roses." Some people say they have even smelled the sweet aroma of roses while praying the rosary. Such is the power of these prayers to pierce the floor of heaven and allow a portion of paradise to seep through.

We can quiet our minds, hearts and souls, breathing in the Holy Spirit, as we let the Rosary beads pass one by one through our fingers. Meditating upon the events of Jesus' life, death and resurrection helps to strengthen the bond between our souls and

God. The mysteries of the Rosary become ever new in our lives each time we open our hearts to the truth that they contain. The Rosary teaches us that those events that happened 2,000 years ago are meant for us, right here and right now.

May we never take for granted the great gift we have been given in this extraordinary prayer.

THE JOYFUL MYSTERIES

1.

THE ANNUNCIATION

"May it be done to me." Luke 1:38

We can only imagine how astonished Mary must have been when the angel Gabriel visited her with such amazing news – that she was going to be the Mother of God. She must have wondered why she was chosen by God Himself for such a monumental role in the salvation of the world. She must have wondered how this remarkable event would come to pass since she was a virgin. We can't imagine how frightened that young Jewish teen might have been. But she said yes.

At times, we feel scared, confused or resistant to what God has planned for us. We try to ignore what He is asking of us. There are the day-to-day struggles we face – all the times when it is hard to say yes to God in the small things, like when we have to fulfill some responsibility, but all we want to do is rest or hang out with friends.

And then there are times God is calling us to something bigger, something that will affect our entire lives and those around us. At times like these, we might feel tempted to ignore God's call and not trust in the Lord, because His plan for us might not be what we had in mind, or it might seem too difficult. It is in these times that we need courage and strength to say yes to God.

In the next several years, we will be making many important decisions that will set a path for our lives. We need to place our trust in God, confident that He knows what is best for us and for our future, which we cannot see, but He can. We need to pray for wisdom to know what course to take.

After the initial shock and fear, we can imagine Mary felt a great joy at having been chosen by God for such a privileged role — to be mother of the redeemer. That joy only came to her because she accepted God's will and placed herself at His service. God has a unique plan for each of us too, a role that can only be filled by one person. If we always say yes to God and try to please Him, we too will have joy like Mary's — a joy that nothing in the world can take away.

2.

THE VISITATION

"At the moment the sound of your greeting reached my ears, the infant in my womb leaped for joy."   Luke 1:44

With Jesus in her womb, Mary set out on a journey. She had learned from the angel Gabriel that her aging cousin Elizabeth was also pregnant, and Mary wanted to be of assistance. Elizabeth greeted Mary with the title, "mother of my Lord" because she knew that the life inside Mary was the one true Lord, the one sent from God. Hidden within Elizabeth's womb, John the Baptist leaped for joy. Even he realized the great presence. Yet to be born himself, John already knew that God was in his midst.

There is someone great within every pregnant woman's womb, someone who can change the world, but we so often don't recognize it, and so many babies die because society fails to see the humanity and great purpose of the unborn child. We are all children of God, all important in His eyes, even if not in the eyes of the world.

John the Baptist's recognition of the Messiah is really amazing when we consider how often we fail to recognize Jesus in our lives. Sometimes, when something bad happens, we do not feel like Jesus is watching over us. We fail to see Him in our times of trial, fail to see how He carries us.

There are also times when He comes to us for help and we fail to recognize Him. When given the opportunity to help those in need, like the hungry or poor, the sad and the lonely, we feel like we're too busy or we simply don't care about someone else's problems.

We encounter Jesus all the time, but He is hidden from our sight, like He was hidden from John the Baptist. He was there in a very real way within Mary's womb, but would we have known He was there? Do we recognize Him when He comes to us each Sunday, very real, yet hidden? We often don't recognize Jesus in the Eucharist because our minds are on other things while we are at Mass. We get distracted by thoughts that are much less important than being with Him.

May we persevere in love for Him, look for Him in all His many "disguises," and stay focused on Him. Then, we can truly say, as Mary did, while visiting Elizabeth, "my soul magnifies the Lord and my spirit rejoices in God my savior."

3.

THE NATIVITY

"You will find an infant wrapped in swaddling clothes and lying in a manger."   Luke 2:12

Jesus, the awesome and powerful God, did not merely humble Himself by joining in our unworthy human nature. He lowered Himself by becoming man in the poorest of conditions. God could have chosen to come as a worldly prince, but He instead was born among poor shepherds and stable animals. The poverty that surrounds the Nativity scene reminds us that God is attracted to the poor, the humble, and the forgotten. Surrendering all pride, we feel compelled to lower ourselves and adore our Lord just as the animals, shepherds, and wise men bowed before the manger.

Even the thought of gazing at that tiny little one, lying in a manger on a bed of hay, can fill us with a deep peace and love for Him. If we had been among the privileged few standing there in that stable that holy night, maybe we would have sensed that there was something different and special about this baby. Would we have known, deep in our soul, that tiny and helpless baby was actually the Son of God? How amazing that He would go to such extremes to become human in order to redeem us. God, the king above all things, born inside a stable, was laid in a feeding trough for the animals, who were probably surprised to find a tiny child in their manger.

How blessed Mary was! Imagine being the one to wrap Him in swaddling clothes and hold Him close to your heart. Joseph had to be the proudest of fathers, for he had been chosen to be the guardian of God the Son. The two new parents must have felt so much emotion and beauty, being truly in the presence of God.

We too have the privilege of being in the true presence of God. When we go into a Catholic Church and the sanctuary lamp is burning beside the Tabernacle, we know that Jesus is really inside, hidden in the bread. In the little stable, Our Lord was born as a defenseless baby, depending entirely upon the care of His devoted parents. In a similar way, Jesus humbles Himself when He comes to us in the Eucharist, as a vulnerable host, often subject to irreverence and desecration. Like Mary and Joseph, we must be protectors of our humble Lord, and thank Him for becoming truly present to us during each Mass and remaining with us in the Tabernacle, just as He was present in Bethlehem at the Nativity.

The shepherds must have been an interesting sight that night, crowding into the stable to pay homage to the young Prince of Peace. We might imagine that one of them lifted a lamb from his shoulders and placed it before the child, who smiled and reached out His hand as the lamb meekly approached its new king. We can be like that shepherd, offering our gifts and hard work to the baby Jesus so that He may take delight in the fruit of our efforts. Whenever we are working — at school, on a job or at home — may we always remember to do everything for Jesus. May we direct all our efforts to the greater glory of God, and try to make sure that whatever we do pleases Him.

4.

THE PRESENTATION

"They took him up to Jerusalem to present him to the Lord."

Luke 2:22

Jesus' parents were obediently following the customs of their faith when they brought Him to the Temple forty days after His birth to dedicate Him to the Lord. It is what Jewish parents did with their first-born sons.

At the Temple that day was a prophet named Simeon. He had waited for this moment — waited for the coming of the Messiah — all his life. God spoke to Simeon's heart and allowed him to sense the presence of the Son of God. The Holy Spirit must have entered his soul and pointed out the humble family from Nazareth, with their simple offering of two turtledoves, among the many other affluent people with their greater offerings of sheep and oxen.

The holy family teaches us the virtues of obedience and humility and the value of poverty — possessing nothing but God Himself. It's very easy to get caught up in the worldly view of money and material things, wishing for the newest electronic devices, trying to keep up with the latest fashion trends, dreaming of owning the fastest car. But we know Jesus is our only true treasure. We learn from Joseph and Mary that Jesus is all we need to have joy. Simeon, too, discovered this. When the aged prophet held the baby Jesus tenderly in his arms, he was filled with an overwhelming joy and serenity and was finally able to be at peace after his many years of waiting for the Messiah. "Now, Master, you may let your servant go in peace, according to your word, for my eyes have seen your salvation..." Seeing the Messiah was the most important thing in Simeon's life. It is what He lived for. It should be what we live for as well. We can see Him in so many places today — whenever we do what pleases Him, whenever we lift our hearts toward Heaven, He is there. He is there in a very special way at Church, in the Blessed Sacrament, giving us His body and blood. God is truly with us, just as He was with Simeon in the Temple that day.

5.

FINDING JESUS IN THE TEMPLE

"When his parents saw him, they were astonished, and his mother said to him, "Son, why have you done this to us? Your father and I have been looking for you with great anxiety." And he said to them, "Why were you looking for me? Did you not know that I must be in my Father's House?" Luke 2:48-49

If you've ever been in a store or some other public place when a child gets lost, you can feel the fear in your gut as the parent frantically searches for the child, terrified of what harm might befall the little one. The reunion is always joyous for everyone, even the bystanders who don't even know the family.

When found, the child is usually almost as relieved as the parent. Children usually fear they won't be found as much as parents fear not finding them. But Jesus, left behind for three days as a boy, was not at all disturbed, because He wasn't really lost. He knew He was right where He was supposed to be: in His Father's house. He was home.

After Mary and Joseph found Him there in the Temple, talking with the teachers, who were amazed at all He had to say, Jesus returned to Nazareth with His parents and was obedient to them. He was King of the universe. He did not have to be obedient to anyone. In the only story of Jesus' childhood, Scripture stresses this virtue, perhaps to show us the importance of obedience to our parents. As teenagers, we may think that we want total independence, but God often speaks to us through others. By obedience we cooperate with His will. Our teenage years are integral in forming the adults that we will become. We must mature in Christ, growing into holy, virtuous people through obedience to those who love and care most for us, namely our earthly parents and our Heavenly Father.

It is not always easy for us to be obedient. It often means doing something we don't want to do or refraining from something we're not allowed to do. But parents know what's best and only want the best for us.

That's why God gives us the command: "Honor your father and mother." Our friends may not always understand this. The world often does not understand why we Christians deny material comforts or "good times" or why we strive to attain holiness. When we spend time in church, people may criticize us or tell us we are wasting time. Prayer time can be viewed as unproductive. We can't see the good that it is accomplishing, but not a split second of any prayer from our heart to God's is ever wasted.

At our age, it is probably rare for us to get lost anymore, at least physically. But we must be on guard not to get lost spiritually, which is even worse. It is so easy to get caught up in the pursuits and pleasures of the world. We must constantly remind ourselves we were made to live in our Father's house, where we can be close to Christ and have true joy, in this life and the next.

THE
LUMINOUS
MYSTERIES

1.

THE BAPTISM OF JESUS

"After Jesus was baptized, he came up from the water and behold, the heavens were opened for him, and he saw the Spirit of God descending like a dove and coming upon him."

Matthew 3:16

What a great privilege for John to baptize Jesus. He knew Jesus was the Messiah. How does someone respond to the privilege of baptizing God? Clearly, it should have been Jesus baptizing John, not the other way around. John said he wasn't even worthy to untie Jesus' sandals. He felt he was so lowly compared to the one who was going to save, not just Israel, but the whole world. We can only imagine the awe John must have felt.

There are things God permits us to do that are such an amazing privilege that we, too, should feel complete and utter awe. That He would count us worthy to receive Him in Holy Communion is perhaps the most remarkable mystery of all human history. Saint Maximilian Kolbe said, "If Angels could be jealous of men, they would be so for one reason: Holy Communion." Jesus allows us the privilege of becoming one with Him, the privilege of making our soul a dwelling place for Him.

But Jesus wasn't asking John to baptize Him merely to give John a gift. He was giving us a gift as well. He was setting an example for us. He knew we needed Baptism. It was a great act of humility for Jesus, who was without sin, to be baptized, so that we who are sinful would follow His example and be saved.

When we were Baptized, our parents offered our lives and souls to God, asking Him to make us heirs to His kingdom. Our Baptism made an indelible mark on our souls, setting us apart for God, so no matter what happens to us in our lives, we are His and we always will be.

Baptism welcomes us into God's family and makes us members of the Church, which will shepherd us the rest of our lives toward Heaven. Baptism lets the Holy Spirit into our hearts and souls, cleansing us from original sin. It is a truly miraculous moment, but too often, we take it for granted. Maybe it happened too long ago for us to remember it. Maybe it seems commonplace. Because so many people are baptized, we don't understand how special it is.

This is my beloved son, in whom I am well pleased. This is what God the Father said as Jesus' was baptized. This is maybe how He feels about all of us at that moment when the waters of baptism wash us clean and make us new. May our one desire be to make sure He remains pleased with us, every moment of every day.

2.

THE WEDDING FEAST AT CANA

"When the wine ran short, the mother of Jesus said to him, 'They have no wine.' And Jesus said to her, 'Woman, how does your concern affect me? My hour has not yet come.' His mother said to the servers, 'Do whatever he tells you.'"

John 2:3-5

Mary knew that the family hosting the wedding she and Jesus were attending was about to face embarrassment at having underestimated the amount of wine needed for all the guests. Back in Jesus' times, wine was very important at weddings.

Jesus didn't immediately agree to help when His mother told Him, "they have no wine." Up until that moment, Jesus had lived a private life. He had not performed any miracles. He told her, "my hour has not yet come." He wasn't being disrespectful to His mother, only telling her of the "problem" with the timing of her request. Still, she didn't get dismayed, and simply directed the waiters to do whatever He said, knowing He would do whatever is right. Mary might not have known that her request would result in Jesus' first miracle, but she knew He could somehow help.

May we, too, always have faith in Jesus in whatever struggles we are facing. He will help us one way or another. Just as Jesus and Mary cared about a shortage of wine at a wedding, they care about every little detail of our lives.

Mary's words are not only for the waiters, but for us too: "Do whatever He tells you." Whatever He tells us will be the right thing, and something good will result. If we do as the waiters did, we will have our every need met. And we might even see miracles too.

3.

THE PROCLAMATION OF THE KINGDOM

"After John had been arrested, Jesus came to Galilee proclaiming the gospel of God: 'This is the time of fulfillment. The kingdom of God is at hand. Repent, and believe in the gospel.'"

Mark 1:14-15

When we think of a kingdom, simplicity and humility may not typically come to mind. But there is nothing typical about the way God does things. So, when Jesus speaks of the Kingdom of God, He is going to send some surprises our way.

Only the most humble, simple and innocent can enter the Kingdom that Jesus tells us about in the Scriptures. Those who are not trying to be first will be first. Those who are not trying to be the greatest in this world will be the greatest in the kingdom of God. Those who give up all the passing pleasures that the world promotes will have true and eternal happiness in the kingdom.

Imagine the splendor of heaven, where God has created a specific place for each of us. St. Paul says, "eye has not seen, nor has ear heard, nor has it entered into the heart of man what God has prepared for those who love Him." In heaven, we will have no worries or fears, only the joy of being with someone we love and who loves us beyond all imagining.

We pray for the coming of the Kingdom every time we pray the Our Father, and by doing so, we pray for holiness. It is difficult to petition God to let "thy kingdom come" if we are attached to our sins. We may instead want God to hold off a little longer in coming so that we can prolong our time of doing the things God does not want us to do. If we are constantly waiting to repent, Jesus' coming for the final judgment will always be something to fear, as will our own death. Jesus beckons us to repent and believe in Him right now, so that we are completely prepared for the time of fulfillment. In turning to the Sacrament of Reconciliation, we can open ourselves to our merciful Father and accept the grace of His forgiveness given so generously to us in Confession. Like the Prodigal Son, we should run into our father's open arms and accept his loving embrace since He is always willing to forgive our offenses. Only when we purify our souls and become innocent children of God will we truly look forward to the coming of the kingdom.

We will experience the fullness of the Kingdom of God only when we get to heaven. But even here and now, the Kingdom of God is among us because Jesus brought it to us when He came down from heaven and became man. Just as the Galileans were in the presence of the kingdom when Christ was with them, we are in the midst of the kingdom when Christ comes to us as heavenly food, the Eucharist. "I am with you always until the end of the age," He told His disciples. Jesus comes to us in the Eucharist each time we attend Mass and watches over us every moment of every day. He is always there protecting us, guarding us, guiding us. Having Him with us means we are already subjects in the kingdom if only we try our best to love and please Him.

4.

THE TRANSFIGURATION

"Jesus took with him Peter, James, and John ... and led them up a high mountain by themselves. And he was transfigured before them; his face shone like the sun and his clothes became white as light ... behold, a bright cloud cast a shadow over them, then from the cloud came a voice that said, "This is my beloved Son, with whom I am well pleased; listen to him." When the disciples heard this, they fell prostrate and were very much afraid. But Jesus came and touched them, saying, "Rise, and do not be afraid."

Matthew 17:1-7

We can be sure that Peter, James and John had seen many amazing things since they had begun to follow Jesus. But they had never seen anything like what they witnessed at the Transfiguration. The Light of the world literally shone before them, giving them a glimpse into eternity. Jesus' transfiguration foreshadows what we will become in heaven.

This mystery shows us how important it is to follow Jesus. We do not want to pass up the glory and beauty of something so magnificent and everlasting just to try to make ourselves happy for a short time on earth. We want to remember, instead, our eternal goal and do what is pleasing to the Lord.

At the Transfiguration, God the Father spoke from heaven: This is my beloved Son, with whom I am well-pleased. Listen to Him." This is our sign to do all we can to achieve holiness, so we can be with Jesus. Like Moses and Elijah, who were honored to stand at His left and His right, maybe we can have that honor when we go to heaven, if only we listen to Him now. Jesus wants us beside Him. That's why He went to such great lengths, enduring such pain and suffering, to snatch us from the darkness and bring us into the light.

If we always stand by Jesus, we will never be lost. His light will illuminate everything for us, and we won't have to wonder what is true or what is right.

The world rejects moral law, but people guided by the Church can discern what is true. Clothed in the Light of Christ, the Church guides us to the truths that the world denies, but the children of God gladly embrace because they know it leads to lasting joy.

5.

THE INSTITUTION OF THE HOLY EUCHARIST

"Jesus took bread, said the blessing, broke it and giving it to his disciples, said, 'Take and eat. This is my body.' Then he took a cup, gave thanks and gave it to them, saying, 'drink from it, all of you, for this is my blood of the Covenant, which will be shed on behalf of many for the forgiveness of sins.'"

Matthew 26:26-28

Receiving Communion is the most intimate moment we have with Jesus. He is physically inside of us. There is no way to get closer to someone than that. We all long for intimacy, to be united with someone we love and who loves us. The Eucharist, the consecrated bread we eat, is Jesus Himself. He gives Himself to us.

It is beautiful that Jesus chooses to be with us in this way. He could have chosen another way — something bigger, more important. Something grander. But Jesus is humble. He chose bread, perhaps because of the simplicity and humility of it.

This incredible gift Jesus gives us is too often taken for granted. He is giving us His body and blood. We can receive Him every day if we wish. We don't always appreciate how precious a gift this is, freely available to us.

We may not always be in a spiritual rapture when we receive Jesus in Communion, but we need to remember what we are receiving is not just bread and wine. It is really the flesh and blood of the savior who died on a cross so we could go to heaven. He gave us Himself in this special way so that we could have Him with us every day on our earthly journey.

This just proves how much He loves us. He doesn't want to leave us on our own. He wants to give us Himself. Jesus, of course, is always with us in spirit. He is always in our presence. He will always be there to help us through our trials and triumphs. But in the Eucharist, He remains with us in a special way, both body and spirit. He will be with us until the end of our days. No matter what, in easy and in hard times. There is no greater gift than that.

THE
SORROWFUL
MYSTERIES

1.

AGONY IN THE GARDEN

"Not my will, but yours be done."
Luke 22:42

Jesus' prayer in the Garden of Gethsemane, becomes very personal for us when we begin to understand that our Lord suffered for each one of us individually, in order to free us from each one of our sins. "My Father, if it is possible, let this cup pass from Me," Jesus prayed before His passion, "yet not as I will, but as You will." Every time we sin, we add to the cup of Jesus' sufferings. Jesus died two thousand years ago for all the sins that would be committed throughout the history of the world. So it is possible for us to lighten His burden by avoiding future sins. Since God stands outside time, we still have the power to change the suffering Jesus had to endure. When we are truly sorry and make a good Confession, all of the sins of our past are wiped away. But how will we resist sin in the future, to avoid adding any more suffering to Jesus' cup? We look to Jesus Himself for the answer, and do what He did: we pray. This is how our love for God grows. This is where we find our strength.

We badly need time in prayer because it takes great strength to stand by Jesus. Everywhere we look, we see people doing things that look fun and enticing. The culture seeks to draw us in, offering instant gratification. We want to enjoy life. But enjoying life is often different from having joy. Sin can be very enjoyable. But only for a fleeting moment. Afterwards, it's not fun at all. It leaves us empty. We have lost something precious and everlasting, trading it in for a moment of fun.

If we don't have a good prayer life, where will we find the strength to resist temptation? Prayer will keep us from falling prey to the lies the world tells us about what will make us happy. But prayer requires discipline. We'll never have time if we don't make the time. We have to make time for prayer like we make time for a shower or to eat. We can begin and end our day in prayer, but is God calling us to even more? He is not just with us twice a day. He is with us always. We can offer little prayers throughout the day, praising God or asking for help or asking how we can serve Him. In this way, we can bring great comfort to our Lord, who suffered and died for us and seeks nothing in return but our love.

2.

THE SCOURGING AT THE PILLAR

"By His stripes we were healed."
Isaiah 53:5

It has long been held that our Lord suffered the scourging specifically to take away our sins against purity. So much in our culture lures us away from God and into thoughts and beliefs that will ultimately cause us to commit sins of impurity. Those harmful messages and images come at us at every turn, through music, movies, TV shows, commercials, books and the internet.

Many of us struggle with temptations to impurity. We can pray and ask Mary for help. She is the model of purity. She remained a virgin forever. Mary was a teen at the Annunciation, when she gave her "yes" to God's plan, though it was different from her own. When we feel tempted to commit sin, we can think about what Mary would do if faced with the struggles we are facing. She always did what God wanted.

In our world today, we have to be vigilant and even strict with ourselves to avoid temptations. It is not an easy task these days, but we should seek out clean entertainment and not accept anything as OK just because it has only a "little bit" of impurity. When we accept a little, it becomes easy to accept more. It is necessary to censor what we see and hear, and we should go out of our way to support media that attempts to oppose the damaging messages that seek to destroy our souls by robbing us of our innocence. We should avoid unknown websites or those we know might have inappropriate content. We owe it to ourselves to ask our parents' guidance in investigating the content of movies and TV shows before watching them. We should turn off songs that send the wrong messages. That's not always easy to do when we enjoy a song for its catchy beat or intriguing melody, but we know it pleases God when we sacrifice those things for our beliefs and morals.

Sometimes following Christ might require us to tell our friends we cannot go with them to see a certain movie. That will take courage, but it will allow us to witness the truth to them, as well as keep ourselves from being bombarded with bad messages or images that are going to stay in our heads and tempt us for a long time to come.

Having the strength to say no to our friends requires a strong prayer life. We aren't going to want to seem weird to our friends. But ultimately, we have to remember we are trying to please God. Pleasing others too often takes precedence in our lives because our friends are tangible to us – they are standing right in front of us. We can hear and see them. We can't hear and see Jesus. Sadly, it is easy to forget the person who suffered so severely for us, who gave His life for us, who loves us more than anyone else ever could. May we pray all the harder and give special attention to making sure we always recall Jesus' presence with us and try to please Him above all others.

3.

THE CROWNING WITH THORNS

"Weaving a crown of thorns, they placed it on his head and a reed in his right hand. And kneeling before him, they mocked him, saying, 'Hail, King of the Jews!' They spat upon him..."

Matthew 27:29-30

Today, we witness so many people treating Jesus like the soldiers treated Him when they placed a crown of thorns on His head and mockingly called Him a king. We hear the Lord's name taken in vain too many times to count. Often His name, which should only be uttered in praise, love, thanks and sincere supplication, is used in anger or flippant exclamations that pair the holy with the defiled. Each time we hear this, we can say a short prayer, telling Jesus how much we love Him. We can bow our heads at the name of the Lord, to show our love and respect for Him and make up for the wrong being done to Him by those who don't know better. Maybe in this way, all the harm can be turned to good. Maybe we would not have thought of God at that moment if someone had not taken His name in vain, but now that He has been called to mind, we can take that moment to adore Him.

St. Dominic Savio would bow his head and say, "blessed be the Name of Jesus," if he heard someone take the Lord's name in vain. One time, he approached a man who had just blasphemed and asked for directions. The man was unable to help, so Dominic asked if he would do him another favor: refrain from letting his temper get the best of him and lead him to blasphemy. The man was moved by the request of this gentle youth and promised to work on this fault. There may be times when we may wish to take our friends aside and kindly tell them that the Lord's name is holy and has no place intermixed with vulgar or slang expressions.

It may seem like we would need a lot of courage to do what Dominic Savio did, but teens do listen to each other's advice and follow each other's examples, so we should not doubt that we can have a positive impact on our friends. God calls us to live our lives in a way that will change others. May they always see us living out our lives with love, so that they may want to investigate the source of that love and be lead right to Jesus.

4.

THE CARRYING OF THE CROSS

"As they were going out, they met a Cyrenian named Simon; this man they pressed into service to carry the cross."

Matthew 27:32

Often, our crosses aren't giant, life-or-death struggles. Usually, the cross is in the small stuff, like facing a mountain of homework or having to decline a party invitation because we know there might be bad things happening there. St. Therese of Lisieux accepted and even embraced all the small sufferings as a way of pleasing Jesus. Even the tiniest suffering, if accepted with a joyful attitude, can be profit for our souls.

For most of us, it is not usually second nature to accept our crosses without complaint. Our first inclination is often to gripe. But it does our soul good if we don't complain, and it can do us no good at all, or even harm, if we do.

Sometimes it seems we have to carry our crosses on our own. We feel alone in our suffering. Maybe none of our friends are going through exactly the same struggles we are. We have all felt like our problems are unique at one time or another. But we are never alone.

We are somewhat like Simon of Cyrene, whom the soldiers forced to take up the cross to Calvary, trudging beside that condemned man named Jesus, who had fallen under the weight of the wood. Simon was not aware that it was God walking beside him. Sometimes it may feel like we are all alone. But we can be sure that Jesus, our best friend, is there with us every step of the way.

Suffering is not going to break us. It is going to lift us up. A lot of the suffering that happens on earth is a way of purifying us. Suffering will take us to heaven. If we accept it, it will take time off our Purgatory.

So many times, we blame God for our suffering, even for things we brought on ourselves by refusing to listen to Him. But even when those consequences happen, we can be grateful that we have learned something from our mistakes. Jesus' death on the cross makes it possible for us to start over, with a new purpose of living our lives only to please Him. He died to take our sins away, to free us from whatever chains bind us to our past.

When bad things happen to us that are beyond our control or ability to prevent or fix, we need only remember to trust Him. He is never going to let anything happen that we don't have the strength to withstand. We can be sure that whatever He is asking us to go through will only benefit us.

We should find our joy in being with Jesus, even if it means suffering with Him. Everyone else may say that's our misery. But we know it's our joy. There's nowhere else we would rather be than with Him, who loves us beyond all imagining.

5.

THE CRUCIFIXION

Aware that everything was now finished, in order that the scripture might be fulfilled, Jesus said, "I thirst." There was a vessel filled with common wine. So they put a sponge soaked in wine on a sprig of hyssop and put it up to his mouth. When Jesus had taken the wine, he said, "It is finished." And bowing his head, he handed over the spirit.

John 19: 28-30

When Jesus said, "I thirst," while hanging on the cross, He did not mean only that He was physically thirsty. St. Therese of Lisieux said Jesus thirsted for love. While suffering on the cross, pouring out His blood to save us, He knew a true friend would be hard to find.

So few of Jesus' friends stayed with Him during the crucifixion. Most of them got scared and ran away. We like to think we would have been among the few at the foot of the cross. But would we? We even find it difficult to stand up for Christ in small ways because we don't want to seem strange or lose friends. He gives His life for us, and we aren't willing to give just a little portion of ours for Him.

When we get closer to Christ and learn more about our Faith, we begin to change our ways and see that some of our friends are still doing the things we have come to understand are wrong. They may begin to see differences in us and question why we have changed. We can explain to them that we are different now because we have decided to follow Christ. Not all of the people in our lives will like the changes we have made. Our temptation is to choose our friends over our best friend – the one who suffered and died for us. It's not easy to lose friends, but we might find that we have to distance ourselves from those who will drag us back into sin.

Friends are supposed to help us become the best version of ourselves. We are supposed to do the same for them. That might require us to lovingly point out to each other the things we are doing wrong. It will most definitely require us to live out our faith by example. We will be ineffective at convincing anyone else of their sins if we ourselves are not living moral lives.

It's important for us to know our faith so we can explain the reasons for wanting to avoid sin. We can consult the Catechism of the Catholic Church, read the lives of the saints and ask a good priest to explain things to us so we can pass along our understanding to those we are trying to help. For instance, if a friend wants us to skip Mass to go to the mall, it is useful for us to know why the Church teaches that missing Mass for no good reason is a mortal sin.

Sometimes as we try to live out our beliefs we may feel like we are swimming upstream against an unyielding current. But it is what we are called to do, for the sake of our friends and our best friend, Jesus.

Our Lord is likely more thirsty now than ever because of all the indifference and ingratitude toward Him in our modern times. We can resolve now to be among His few true friends.

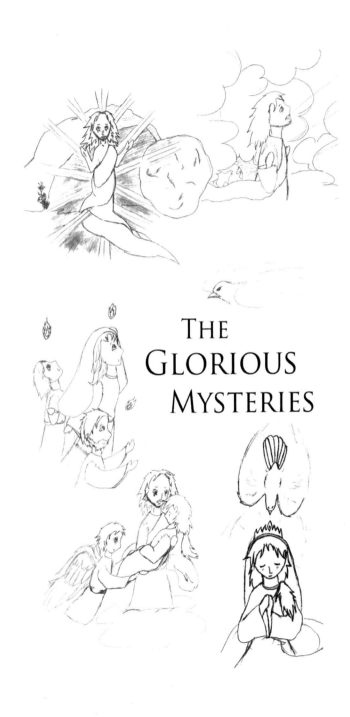

THE
GLORIOUS
MYSTERIES

1.

THE RESURRECTION

"Do not let your hearts be troubled ... In my father's house there are many dwelling places. If there were not, would I have told you that I am going to prepare a place for you? And if I go and prepare a place for you, I will come back again and take you to myself, so that where I am you also may be."

John 14: 1-3

Our lives take on a new meaning if we keep our eyes on the Resurrection. The Resurrection changes everything. It is not only the basis of our faith, but the reason we can rejoice, even when all is not going our way. There is another life after this one. We have eternal life. Jesus suffered. We're going to suffer too. But this life we are living now is not the only life. The Resurrection of Jesus is our promise that we too will rise to eternal life in heaven, where there is only joy, peace and love.

There is one treasure above all others – our faith. But it is often under attack at this time in our lives. We have a lot of information coming at us. We are introduced to so many new ideas and exposed to different view-points. It is important for us to know what our Church teaches and why. There is a reason for every teaching the Church holds dear, and when we find out the reasons, the "rules" start to make sense, and we start to realize they are more than rules. They are a way of life that leads us to perfect love and eternal joy.

There is nothing wrong with having fun, but we aren't seeking fun above all else. We're seeking fulfillment. Maybe it won't come today or tomorrow. We know our purpose here isn't just to have fun. Seeking fun above all else could mess up eternity. We have to deny ourselves some things in this life. Maybe we'll have to decide not to go to a late-night party, for instance, if it means being too tired the next morning to attend Mass. We give up anything that keeps us from uniting ever more closely with Christ because we know that He is our true joy. We avoid drinking, drugs and impurity because we don't want to mess up our earthly lives, of course, but mostly because we don't want to mess up our eternal lives. A lot of choices, such as gossip and viewing immoral movies, might not seem to have serious consequences in this life, but they will affect our path to heaven. These are the things we avoid because we want to please God, not because we are afraid of getting in trouble. We seek His perfect will for our lives, so we can be worthy of the promise of the Resurrection.

2.

THE ASCENSION

"As he blessed them, he parted from them and was taken up to heaven."

Luke 24:51

Jesus came back to be with His friends for forty days before He ascended into heaven. He didn't abandon them. And He never abandons us either. He promised He would be with us forever. And we are grateful because we know how much we need Him. The apostles were afraid to be on their own. They didn't know what persecutions they would face. They were comforted by Jesus' promise to be with them always. It was their reassurance that they weren't going it alone. We have that assurance as well. Jesus will always be there to help us. In the Eucharist, He is literally with us -- body and soul, His real presence among us. But we don't have to wait to go to church to be in conversation with Him. We have the Holy Spirit with us all the time. We can praise Him throughout the day, glorify-ing Him through what we say. He is always present with us in our souls if we are in a state of grace, meaning we don't have unconfessed mortal sin on our souls. We have the Holy Trinity dwelling within us.

Some people advise that, if we want to be good, we should pretend that Jesus is in the room with us. But no pretense is necessary, because Jesus is actually living inside of us! That's why we should never let our souls remain dirty with sin. It is not fair to Jesus when we are giving Him less than the best conditions to dwell in. We should clean up His dwelling place by going to Confession regularly.

But it is not enough to avoid throwing garbage into our souls and letting them remain empty. We should fill our souls with good things, through prayer and praise and participating in the sacraments. If we accept the gifts Jesus bestows on us through the Church, we will hold the comfort of His presence in our heart throughout our lives and one day join Him in Heaven.

3.

THE DESCENT OF THE HOLY SPIRIT

"If you love me, you will keep my command-ments. And I will ask the Father, and He will give you another advocate to be with you always, the Spirit of truth, which the world cannot accept, because it neither sees nor knows it. But you know it, because it remains with you, and will be in you. I will not leave you orphans; I will come to you." John 14:15-17

The Holy Spirit is living inside us. But we are not to keep Him hidden there. We are called to emanate the gifts of the Holy Spirit: wisdom, patience, counsel, fortitude, fear of the Lord, piety, knowledge and understand-ing. This is how the Church is built.

The Church was "born" on the day the Holy Spirit descended on the apostles in the upper room. On Pentecost, the Holy Spirit gave the apostles divine inspiration, strength to preach and courage to evangel-ize. The Holy Spirit has continued to guide the Church for 2,000 years, through the popes and bishops. He guides our individ-ual lives as well, giving us wisdom and knowledge to spread our faith. Much of the witness we give is by example. Our friends know we go to Mass because it comes up in conversation. They know we cherish our faith because they see our crucifix or holy medals. They see us giving of ourselves to help others and they know we have learned compassion from someone. When they see us living out our faith, people may be drawn to our goodness and begin to wonder about the reason for it. When they discover that Jesus is the reason for our joy, they may want to share in that joy and begin to explore the faith. In the same way, when we do something wrong, it makes the Church look bad because people see us as part of the Church.

Sometimes, we are tempted to wait until the "right time" to begin evangelizing. Maybe we decide we will wait until we find our vocation or until we go off to college or until we settle down and have a family. But teens can be a powerful force in society, so waiting just wastes a valuable window of opportunity. We hear stories of families who begin to pray together at the suggestion of a teen family member. Or young people who convert because a friend invited them to church.

We have the gifts of the Holy Spirit to help us spread the faith, just like the first apostles did. May the fire within us burn bright enough to set the world ablaze.

4.

THE ASSUMPTION

"Therefore my heart is glad and my soul rejoices, my body, too, abides in confidence; Because you will not abandon my soul to the nether world, nor will you suffer your faithful one to undergo corruption."

Psalms 16:9-10

Mary followed God's will perfectly. She didn't hold any piece of herself back. Because of this, God gave her a special gift. We won't find Mary in any tomb because her body is in Heaven, along with her soul.

The mystery of the Assumption, when Mary was assumed body and soul into heaven, gives us great hope. We get a glimpse of what lies ahead for us. Mary is sharing completely in what we have to look forward to. When we die, we know that our souls can go to Heaven, but we will not be reunited with our restored bodies until the end of time.

Mary was favored with the Assumption because of her very special role in salvation history. She was the first Tabernacle, as she carried Jesus in her womb for nine months. She was the first human dwelling place for Him, and we share in that gift now as well each time we receive His body and blood into ours in Holy Communion.

At this time in our lives, we are making so many important decisions about our future. One day soon, we will be leaving our parents. If they have succeeded in helping to build a solid foundation and we are already living virtuous lives, we are likely to stay focused on Jesus. But if we are wavering, we will be tempted to do the wrong things more and more as we start to make more of our own decisions. If we keep our eye on how Mary lived her life, in simplicity, humility and obedience, we cannot fail. May we model ourselves after Mary and surrender ourselves entirely to Jesus like she did, so we can join her in heaven someday.

5.

THE CORONATION

"A great sign appeared in the sky, a woman clothed with the sun, with the moon under her feet, and on her head a crown of twelve stars." Revelation 12:1

We see Mary in the Book of Revelation wearing a crown of twelve stars, signifying the twelve tribes of Israel and her queenship over the entire world. After a completely humble earthly life, Mary was crowned queen of heaven and earth. Humility is the finest virtue because it is the opposite of pride, which is the root of all sin. Pride faces inward, taking care of only itself. If we are prideful, everything we do is done to satisfy our own desires. Lucifer's first sin was pride. He was once the brightest angel in heaven. But he wanted to be above God. He told God, "I will not serve."

Whenever we try to use our talents in the way we want instead of the way God would have us use them, we are guilty of the sin of pride. A celebrity, with an incredible voice and a God-given talent to dance, does a disservice to her dignity and eternal happiness by choosing to dress immodestly and sing impure lyrics. Though God gave her the talents, she tells Him, "My time and my talents are mine, and I will do with them what I please. I will not use my gifts for You. I will, instead, use them to hurt You." This, in essence, is what Lucifer said to God after God had given him such great gifts.

We like to think we own our time, we own ourselves, we did something to merit our talents. But there is nothing we would own had God not given it to us. Realizing that is the key to humility. Mary mastered this virtue perfectly. And look what happened to her in heaven, after living a life of humility and sacrifice.

If Mary is queen of heaven and earth, and she is our mother, as Jesus tells us, then we are princes and princesses. We are heirs to the Kingdom. We can be commoners and choose to follow the devil, or we can have great glory reserved for those who love the King. Who would not want to be a prince or a princess? We are going to have to surrender our will, but we will have unimaginable treasures. We get to live in the palace, where all our needs are taken care of. We have no worries. Our Father is the king, after all. We're under His protection. The devil cannot harm us. And Mary, our queen, will help us stay true to our royal calling through her prayers for us and her example of perfect love.

HOW TO PRAY THE ROSARY

1. While holding the crucifix, make the SIGN OF THE CROSS: "In the name of the Father, and of the Son and of the Holy Spirit. Amen."

2. Then, recite the APOSTLE'S CREED:
"I BELIEVE IN GOD, the Father almighty, Creator of heaven and earth, and in Jesus Christ, his only Son, our Lord, who was conceived by the Holy Spirit, born of the Virgin Mary, suffered under Pontius Pilate, was crucified, died and was buried; he descended into hell; on the third day he rose again from the dead; he ascended into heaven, and is seated at the right hand of God the Father almighty; from there he will come to judge the living and the dead. I believe in the Holy Spirit, the Holy Catholic Church, the communion of saints, the forgiveness of sins, the resurrection of the body, and life everlasting. Amen."

3. Recite the OUR FATHER on the first large bead:
"OUR FATHER, Who art in heaven, Hallowed be Thy Name. Thy Kingdom come. Thy Will be done, on earth as it is in Heaven. Give us this day our daily bread. And forgive us our trespasses, as we forgive

those who trespass against us. And lead us not into temptation, but deliver us from evil. Amen."

4. On each of the three small beads, recite a HAIL MARY for the increase of faith, hope and love. "HAIL MARY, full of grace, the Lord is with thee; Blessed art thou among women, and blessed is the fruit of thy womb, Jesus. Holy Mary, Mother of God, pray for us sinners, now and at the hour of death. Amen."

5. Recite the GLORY BE on the next large bead.
"GLORY BE to the Father, and to the Son, and to the Holy Spirit. As it was in the beginning, is now, and ever shall be, world without end. Amen."

6. Recall the first Rosary Mystery and recite the Our Father on the next large bead.

7. On each of the adjacent ten small beads (known as a decade), recite a Hail Mary while reflecting on the mystery.

8. On the next large bead, recite the Glory Be.

9. The FATIMA PRAYER may be said here:

"O MY JESUS, forgive us our sins, save us from the fires of hell, lead all souls to heaven, especially those who are in most need of Thy mercy."

10. Begin the next decade by recalling the next mystery and reciting an Our Father. Move to the small beads and pray ten Hail Marys while meditating on the mystery.

11. Continue until you have circled the entire Rosary (five decades.) Or for a full Rosary, you will circle it four times (twenty decades.)

12. It is customary to CONCLUDE with the following prayers:

HAIL HOLY QUEEN

"HAIL, HOLY QUEEN, mother of mercy, our life, our sweetness, and our hope. To thee do we cry, poor banished children of Eve. To thee do we send up our sighs, mourning and weeping in this valley of tears. Turn then, most gracious advocate, thine eyes of mercy toward us, and after this our exile, show us the blessed fruit of thy womb, Jesus. O clement, O loving, O sweet Virgin Mary.
(Verse) Pray for us, O Holy Mother of God.

(Response) That we may be made worthy of the promises of Christ."

ROSARY PRAYER

(Verse) Let us pray,
(Response) O God, whose only begotten Son, by His life, death, and resurrection, has purchased for us the rewards of eternal salvation, grant, we beseech Thee, that by meditating on these mysteries of the most holy Rosary of the Blessed Virgin Mary, that we may both imitate what they contain and obtain what they promise, through Christ our Lord. Amen.

Most Sacred Heart of Jesus, have mercy on us.

Immaculate Heart of Mary, pray for us.

In the Name of the Father, and of the Son and of the Holy Spirit. Amen.

FICTION AVAILABLE FROM
CARITAS PRESS / CATHOLIC WORD

Sherry Boas' life-changing Lily series, acclaimed as "masterful," "profound," "riveting," "heart-wrenching" and "made for our times."

UNTIL LILY (Book 1)

Bev Greeley could have never predicted that the burden she tried to cast off long ago would become her only source of joy in her final days. A moving story about strife, chaos, tragedy, loss, laughter, redemption and deep meaning possible only when you hand yourself over to love

WHEREVER LILY GOES (Book 2)

Terry Lovely isn't expecting any great rewards for her decision to uproot her family, move halfway across the country and take care of her sister Lily, who has Down Syndrome. But Terry is about to discover that Lily will give more than she will ever take, including a certain something Terry doesn't even know is missing.

LIFE ENTWINED WITH LILY'S (Book 3)

A dark day in Beth Lovely's past casts a mournful shadow over her entire future. And although Beth has revealed her unspeakable secret to no one, her Aunt Lily is unwittingly responsible for a resuscitating breath of new hope.

THE THINGS LILY KNEW (Book 4)

A brilliant Rhodes Scholar whose love life is torn in threes, Annabel Greeley is not lacking in wit or intellect. But when the accomplished geneticist is faced with a decision that will change, not only her life, but the future of humanity, the answers elude her. She is hounded by the ever-present and unavoidable fact that she would not be alive if it weren't for her Aunt Lily, who happened to have Down syndrome and, seemingly, all of life's answers. Annabel's life is about to change in profound and paradoxical ways as she sets out in search of the things Lily knew.

Visit www.LilyTrilogy.com

"Sure to be a Catholic classic...
Magnificent read, highly recommended."
Robert Curtis, Catholic Sun Media Critic

WING TIP
by Sherry Boas

Dante De Luz's steel was forged in his youth, in the crucible of harsh losses and triumphant love. But that steel gets tested like never before as the revelation of a family secret presents the young Catholic priest with the toughest challenge of his life, with stakes that couldn't get any higher.

ROSARY TITLES AVAILABLE FROM
CARITAS PRESS / CATHOLIC WORD

A Mother's Bouquet
Rosary Meditations for Moms

A Father's Heart
Rosary Meditations for Dads

A Child's Treasure
Rosary Meditations for Children

Amazing Love
Rosary Meditations for Teens

Generations of Love
Rosary Meditations for Grandparents

A Servant's Heart
Rosary Meditations for Altar Servers

Visit www.LilyTrilogy.com

www.LilyTrilogy.com

Caritas Press

(602) 920-2846

Email: Sherry@LilyTrilogy.com